SECOND EDITION

TOUCHSTONE

WORKBOOK 4A

T0268559

MICHAEL MCCARTHY

JEANNE MCCARTEN

HELEN SANDIFORD

CAMBRIDGE
UNIVERSITY PRESS

Shaftesbury Road, Cambridge CB2 8EA, United Kingdom

One Liberty Plaza, 20th Floor, New York, NY 10006, USA

477 Williamstown Road, Port Melbourne, VIC 3207, Australia

314–321, 3rd Floor, Plot 3, Splendor Forum, Jasola District Centre, New Delhi – 110025, India

103 Penang Road, #05-06/07, Visioncrest Commercial, Singapore 238467

Cambridge University Press & Assessment is a department of the University of Cambridge.

We share the University's mission to contribute to society through the pursuit of education, learning and research at the highest international levels of excellence.

www.cambridge.org
Information on this title: www.cambridge.org/9781107627086

© Cambridge University Press & Assessment 2005, 2014

This publication is in copyright. Subject to statutory exception and to the provisions of relevant collective licensing agreements, no reproduction of any part may take place without the written permission of Cambridge University Press & Assessment.

First published 2005
Second Edition 2014

20 19 18 17 16 15 14 13 12 11

Printed in Great Britain by Ashford Colour Press Ltd.

A catalog record for this publication is available from the British Library.

ISBN 978-1-107-68043-2 Student's Book
ISBN 978-1-107-62430-6 Student's Book A
ISBN 978-1-107-63748-1 Student's Book B
ISBN 978-1-107-68275-7 Workbook
ISBN 978-1-107-62708-6 Workbook A
ISBN 978-1-107-69602-0 Workbook B
ISBN 978-1-107-66153-2 Full Contact
ISBN 978-1-107-67936-8 Full Contact A
ISBN 978-1-107-66763-1 Full Contact B
ISBN 978-1-107-68151-4 Teacher's Edition with Assessment Audio CD/CD-ROM
ISBN 978-1-107-61272-3 Class Audio CDs (4)

Additional resources for this publication at www.cambridge.org/touchstone2

Cambridge University Press & Assessment has no responsibility for the persistence or accuracy of URLs for external or third-party internet websites referred to in this publication, and does not guarantee that any content on such websites is, or will remain, accurate or appropriate. Information regarding prices, travel timetables, and other factual information given in this work is correct at the time of first printing but Cambridge University Press & Assessment does not guarantee the accuracy of such information thereafter.

Contents

Interesting lives

Lesson A / Interviews

Meet Alex. . . .

Grammar | Claire is interviewing Alex, a successful photographer, for a news website.
Circle the correct verb forms to complete the conversation.

Claire   When **did you start** / **were you starting** taking photos?

Alex   Gosh, **I'm taking** / **I've been taking** photos since I was about six.

Claire   Really? So, what kind of camera **did you use** / **have you used** back then?

Alex   Well, when I was young, my uncle **showed** / **was showing** me how
to use this old camera and how to develop the prints. I still use it!

Claire   That's amazing. So, what projects **do you work** / **are you working**
on currently?

Alex   I just started this nature series. **I'm taking** / **I was taking** photos
of trees. You know, trees that have interesting shapes.

Claire   That's great. How many tree photos **have you taken** /
have you been taking so far?

Alex   A lot. Hundreds.

Claire   Really? And how has your work changed? I mean, what kind of
photography **were you doing** / **have you been doing** five years ago?

Alex   Well, I **was working** / **'ve worked** on some color portraits for a
competition. I **didn't win** / **wasn't winning**, but it was a good experience.

About you 1

Grammar | Write the questions using a correct verb form. Then write true answers.

1. What / you take / photos of lately ? _What have you been taking photos of lately?_
   I've been taking photos of my friends and interesting buildings in my hometown.

2. How long / you / have / a camera ? _____

3. your parents / take / many photos of you when you were a child ? _____

4. you ever / be / to a photographer's studio ? _____

5. When / you last take a photo ? _____

6. What / social networking sites / you / post / your photos on currently ? _____

3 Questions and answers

Grammar | **Complete each conversation with the correct form of the verb given. Sometimes more than one answer is possible.**

1. (watch)

    Ben   What kinds of movies ____*have*____ you _*been watching*_ lately?

    Kumi   Well, mostly I _____ horror movies. I usually _____ three or four horror movies a month. Actually, I _____ a great horror movie last night.

2. (live)

    Ana   _____ you ever _____ in another country?

    Joel   Yes, I _____ in two other countries. I _____ in Canada for three years after I left college, and I _____ in Kenya until last June.

3. (eat)

    Christa   You look great. What's your secret?

    Jalila   Thanks. I _____ a lot of vegetables and whole grains lately. And I always _____ six small meals a day. I just _____ a salad for lunch.

4. (write)

    Vito   How long _____ you _____ poetry?

    Kim   Um. I guess I _____ poetry for about four years. I _____ almost every day if I can. Yesterday, I _____ for almost three hours nonstop!

4 About you 2

Grammar | **Answer the questions with true information.**

1. How long have you been studying English? _I've been studying English for five years.___

2. Have you ever lived in another country? _____

3. What kinds of music are you listening to these days? _____

4. What kinds of TV shows do you watch? _____

5. What did you do during your last vacation? _____

6. What were you doing at this time last week? _____

1 Dream jobs

Grammar
and
vocabulary | Circle the correct words to complete the paragraphs.

1. LEIGH HUDSON tells us how she **seemed** / **ended up** / **decided** being an editor.

Well, after I **imagined / finished / bothered** taking my law school entrance exams, I still wasn't sure if I wanted to be a lawyer. I already had a degree in English and was **considering / expecting / agreeing** training to be a journalist. Then one day, I saw an ad for an editorial assistant on a publishing company's website, and I **offered / expected / decided** to apply for it. After the interview, the manager said I was right for the job and **offered / ended up / considered** to pay me a good salary. I immediately **agreed / finished / missed** to take the job. Anyway, I've been working at the company for over five years, and now I'm a senior editor. I absolutely love my job – I can't **agree / expect / imagine** doing anything else!

2. GEORGE ALLEN explains how he became a chef.

I wasn't really **agreeing / missing / planning on** being a chef. I **spent / bothered / decided** four years in college studying electrical engineering. After I graduated, I **agreed / happened / started** working at an engineering firm and had a great salary, but a lot of responsibility. After six months, I **intend / remember / miss** thinking, "Am I really happy being an electrical engineer?" I decided I wasn't happy at all, so I quit my job and applied to a local cooking school. After I finished training, I opened a small restaurant. I've never **ended up / missed / offered** working at my old job – not once. And that was 15 years ago now!

3. CELIA MENDEZ tells us how she became a dancer.

Well, a few years ago, my friends and I **happened / seemed / missed** to go on vacation to a Caribbean resort that put on a great show every night with singing and dancing and everything. I was taking dance classes at the time, and I was actually **finishing / bothering / considering** becoming a dancer. Anyway, one night, the resort had a talent competition for the guests. I didn't **imagine / happen / bother** to sign up. But my friends said, "Celia, this **seems / spends / expects** to be a perfect opportunity for you. You're such a good dancer. You should do it!" Well, to make a long story short, I won the talent competition, and the resort offered me a position as a dancer! I never **happened / expected / ended up** to be a successful professional dancer, least of all at a Caribbean resort! Dreams really do come true!

2 How I ended up living in New York City

Grammar and vocabulary | **Complete the paragraph with the correct form of the verbs.**

A lot of people ask me how I ended up ___living___ (live)
in New York City. Well, actually, I wasn't planning on _____ (be)
here. It's just that the opportunity came up when my friend Samuela
happened _____ (move) here for college. She needed a roommate,
so I agreed _____ (share) an apartment with her in the city. We were
only in the apartment a couple of months when Samuela started
_____ (miss) home. She said she missed _____ (be) with her family.
I guess she couldn't imagine _____ (stay) three more years
and _____ (be) happy. So, she decided _____ (complete) the
semester, and then she transferred to a college back home. Anyway,
I kept the apartment and found a great job. I've been here for over
six years now, but Samuela and I are still great friends. We've never
stopped _____ (email) each other, and we call each other all the
time. We just live in different cities – that's all!

3 About you

Grammar and vocabulary | **Answer the questions with true information.**

1. Where do you think you'll end up living in a few years?
   I think I'll end up living in Paris after I finish school.

2. What are you planning on doing when you finish this English course?
   _____

3. Have you started reading a new book recently?
   _____

4. What's something fun you remember doing as a child?
   _____

5. Have you ever decided to do something and then regretted it?
   _____

6. Do you expect to get a good grade in this class?
   _____

7. What do you intend to do this weekend?
   _____

8. Is there anything you can't imagine doing in life?
   _____

We're both getting scared. . . .

1 When I was little, . . .

Conversation strategies | **Read the conversation. Change the underlined verbs to the simple present to highlight the key moments.**

Freda   This pie reminds me of the time my sister made me eat a mud pie.

Chris   You're kidding! What happened?

Freda   Well, when I was very little, she and I used to play together, and we would always play outside, you know?

Chris   Yeah. We always played outside, too. Not like kids nowadays.

Freda   Well, anyway, one day, I <u>was</u> ⸢'m / am⸣ in the yard, and she <u>made</u> me eat a mud pie. Here she <u>was</u>, seven years old, in the yard with three beautiful mud pies. She <u>said</u>, "Freda, try this. It's so good." And she <u>acted</u> like she put some in her mouth. I was three years old, so what did I know?

Chris   Oh, no! What did it taste like?

Freda   I don't remember.

Chris   Really?

Freda   No. But I remember being sick afterward.

2 I'll never forget . . .

Conversation strategies | **Read the conversation. Change some verbs in Sarah's story to the simple present or present continuous to highlight key moments in the story.**

Sarah   Did I ever tell you about the time I ran out of cash in South Korea?

Lisa   No. What happened?

Sarah   Well, I was traveling through South Korea, way out in the middle of nowhere, and I ~~ran out~~ ⸢run out⸣ of cash and I had no way of getting back to Seoul.

Lisa   Really? You didn't have any traveler's checks or anything?

Sarah   Well, I had one check for 50 dollars, but I was in the mountains, and there was nowhere to exchange it.

Lisa   Oh, no! So, what did you do?

Sarah   Well, I was getting pretty nervous. I was walking around and couldn't find a bank or anything. Anyway, finally, I met this really nice French man. So I explained the situation, and he agreed to take my traveler's check in exchange for Korean money. So at least I had enough money to get a bus to the nearest town. And so yeah, I went to the most expensive hotel.

Lisa   Why the most expensive hotel?

Sarah   Well, back then, small hotels didn't accept credit cards. And it was a holiday, so the banks were closed.

Lisa   So you stayed there?

Sarah   Yeah. I ended up booking a room for the night, and then the next day, I found a bank and got some cash. So it all worked out in the end.

3 This great bike path

Conversation strategies Complete the story with *this* or *these*.

My friends went bike riding one day on ____*this*____ great bike path in the country. The bike path is really _____ old railroad track that isn't used by trains anymore. Anyway, it goes through all _____ beautiful old farms. But, you see, my friends are from the city, so they're not used to seeing farm animals and fields and stuff. So, my friends are riding along, and they see all _____ goats in a field. Well, they stop to take photos, but they have no idea that goats can be a little unfriendly. Suddenly, they see _____ big goat running toward them, so they jump back on their bikes and ride away, you know, really quickly. Then _____ guy starts yelling at them. It turns out it's the farmer, and they're riding their bikes on his field.

4 Really?

Conversation strategies Rewrite these stories. Use the simple present or present continuous to highlight some key moments in each story. Use *this* and *these* to highlight important people, things, or events.

1. You know, a friend of mine is always seeing famous people when she's out. One time, she was checking out a computer in a computer store. And all of a sudden, she looked up and saw her favorite basketball player. He was standing next to her – checking out the same computer!

   You know, this friend of mine is always seeing famous people when she's out.
   One time, she was checking out this computer in a computer store. And all
   of a sudden, . . .

2. You know, my cousin Adam met his fiancée because of his dog. He has an enormous dog named Scruffy. Well, one day they were in the park. Anyway, Scruffy started chasing a squirrel and pulled my cousin right into a woman. So, Adam apologized, and he and the woman started talking. And to make a long story short, now they're engaged!

   _____

   _____

   _____

3. I remember one time my friend Linda had a party. It was for her graduation, I think, and we were all outdoors. Anyway, the weather was beautiful at first, but after an hour or so, some dark clouds started coming in, and it started to rain really hard. So, she just turned on a radio, and we all started dancing in the rain. We had so much fun. It was the best party ever.

   _____

   _____

   _____

1 Super man

Reading **A** Read the article. What do you think an *activist* is?

☐ a successful actor   ☐ a motivational speaker
☐ someone who is physically active   ☐ someone who works for a cause

Inspiring in Life and Death

Until 1995, Christopher Reeve was living a life most people only dream about. He was a successful actor – famous for his roles in the *Superman* movies – and happily married with three children. He had everything to live for.

Then on May 27, 1995, his life changed dramatically. Reeve fell off his horse while riding in a horse-jumping competition. The accident left him with serious injuries – a fracture in the second vertebra of his neck – and Reeve was left paralyzed from his neck down.

Reeve was confined to a wheelchair and had to depend on his wife, nurses, doctors, and therapists to do everything for him. He could no longer walk, hold anything in his hands, or feed or wash himself. He also relied on a respirator to help him breathe.

Many people may have given up hope and felt sorry for themselves. But not Christopher Reeve.

Shortly after his accident, Reeve said, "The only limits you have are the ones you put on yourself." With this positive attitude, he began adjusting to his new life.

Amazingly, he continued to act in movies and direct them. But most importantly, he became an activist for people with spinal cord injuries. He raised money for research and started the Christopher & Dana Reeve Foundation, which awards money to people researching cures for paralysis. He wrote an autobiography, *Still Me*. He even testified before the U.S. Senate to encourage funding for stem-cell research.

Although Reeve never recovered from his injuries, he remained hopeful throughout his life about finding a cure for paralysis. By not giving up hope, he gave other people with disabilities hope that in the future, recovery won't be against all odds.

Christopher Reeve
September 25, 1952–October 10, 2004

B Read the article again. Then answer the questions.

1. What movies did Christopher Reeve star in? _____

2. What was Reeve doing when he hurt his neck? _____

3. Who did Reeve have to rely on for help? _____

4. What does the Christopher & Dana Reeve Foundation do? _____

_____

2 How I overcame stage fright

Writing **A** Read the anecdote. Then put the story in the correct order by writing each number in the correct box.

---

1. Set the general time or place.
2. Set the particular time or place.
3. Describe what happened.
4. End the story. Link the events to now.

☐ So, with that memory in my mind, I calmed down and walked on stage. I looked at the audience, and I thought, "I know you want me to do well." I closed my eyes and played a great recital.

☐ Today, remembering my teacher's words helps me to be confident when I perform. And it helps me with a lot of other things, too!

☐ I'm a musician, and when I was in graduate school, I had to give a final violin recital to get my degree. I was nervous because there were so many talented students at my school.

☐ On the night of the recital, I was so nervous that my hands were shaking. But I remembered what my very first teacher said to me years before: "People are here because they want you to do well."

B Use the steps above to write an anecdote about something you were nervous about doing and how you overcame it.

Unit 1 Progress chart

What can you do? Mark the boxes. ✓ = I can . . . ? = I need to review how to . . .	To review, go back to these pages in the Student's Book.
☐ use the simple and continuous forms of verbs.	2 and 3
☐ use verbs that are followed by verb + *-ing* or *to* + verb.	4 and 5
☐ use at least 10 new verbs.	2, 4, and 5
☐ use the present tense to highlight key moments in a story.	6
☐ use *this* and *these* to highlight key people, things, and events.	7
☐ write an anecdote.	9

Grammar

Vocabulary

Conversation strategies

Writing

Personal tastes

Lesson A / Makeovers

1 Confessions of a fashion queen

Grammar and vocabulary | Complete the sentences with the words in the box.

| hard | important | much | nice | ✓often | quickly |

1. I go shopping as _often_ as I can. I go almost every other day.
2. You can't look your best if you get ready as _____ as possible. It's better to take your time.
3. Jeans can look just as _____ as pants if you wear them with a cool top.
4. For me, comfort isn't as _____ as style when it comes to choosing clothes.
5. I try as _____ as I can to look great every day. I pay a lot of attention to how I look.
6. I don't like bright colors as _____ as dark colors. I almost always wear black.

2 Dear Vera, . . .

Grammar and vocabulary | Complete the letters with the words and expressions in the box.

| fast | ✓interested in fashion | little time | many things | much attention | scruffy |

❶ Dear Vera,

My boyfriend isn't as _interested in fashion_ as I am, and he wears the same clothes all the time. He really needs a makeover. How can I help him look better? – *JB, Vancouver*

Dear JB,

Lots of people don't pay as _____ to their appearance as their partners would like. Gently let your boyfriend know that you want to help him look better. Help him pick out clothes that aren't as _____ as the ones he wears now. Your boyfriend might not want your help at first, but he'll be glad when people start noticing how good he looks. – *Vera*

❷ Dear Vera,

It takes me so long to get ready in the morning, and I always end up being late for work. I need to get ready as _____ as possible. What should I do? – *CN, Taipei*

Dear CN,

Mornings are always difficult. You need to spend as _____ as possible organizing yourself. So, to save time, do as _____ as you can the night before. Pick out your clothes before you go to bed, and put everything you need for the day in your bag. That way, your mornings won't be as rushed. – *Vera*

3 She isn't as . . .

Look at the pictures of Sachi and Nell. How are they alike or different? Write sentences with
as . . . as or *not as . . . as.*

1. (tall) *Sachi isn't as tall as Nell.* _____

   _____

2. (hair / short) _____

   _____

3. (many dark clothes) _____

   _____

4. (skirt / long) _____

   _____

5. (shoes / comfortable) _____

   _____

6. (much jewelry) _____

   _____

7. (earrings / big) _____

   _____

8. They both love fashion. (interested in fashion)

   _____

   _____

4 About you

Answer the questions with true information. Use *as . . . as* or *not as . . . as.*

1. Do you generally wear bright colors as often as dark colors?
   I don't wear bright colors as often as dark colors. I'm most comfortable in black. _____

2. Do you spend as much money on clothes as your friends?

   _____

3. Do you try as hard as you can to be trendy and fashionable?

   _____

4. Do you have as many accessories as your best friend?

   _____

5. Do your parents care as much about their appearance as you do?

   _____

6. Do you find stylish clothes to be as comfortable as casual clothes?

   _____

7. Do you spend as little time as possible getting ready in the morning?

   _____

1 Isn't that dress awful?

Grammar | **Complete the conversations with *isn't, aren't, don't,* or *doesn't*.**

1. A Oh, look at that dress. ___Isn't___ it awful?
   B Oh, I don't know. It's what's in style. _____ you interested in fashion?
   A Not really. Are you?
   B Kind of. But look at this dress. _____ it have something special about it?
   A Yeah, it has something all right – a $5,000 price tag! _____ that a little expensive for a dress?
   B Yeah. But being fashionable isn't cheap.

2. A Are you ready yet?
   B Yes, almost. I . . . um . . . just need to find a tie.
   A _____ you have lots of ties?
   B Yeah, but they're all dirty.
   A You should wear a jacket, too, _____ you think?
   B But it's warm outside. _____ this outfit look good?
   A Well, . . . um, _____ your socks different colors?
   B Oh, yeah. You're right. I need to find socks now, too!

2 Don't you think . . . ?

Grammar | **Rewrite the sentences as negative questions.**

1. Leather jackets are cool.
   Aren't leather jackets cool?

2. Most sneakers cost way too much nowadays.
   _____

3. A tie is a great way to complete a man's outfit.
   _____

4. Plaid looks great with floral prints.
   _____

5. It's hard to find jeans that fit well.
   _____

6. Neon green and orange are great colors.
   _____

③ What's in fashion?

Vocabulary | **A** Look at the picture and read the comments. Two things in each description are wrong. Underline the wrong word(s) and correct the sentences.

1. Luis looks very stylish in his denim jeans and a <u>short-sleeved</u> shirt. His <u>neon</u> <u>striped</u> tie looks cool, too.

   Luis looks very stylish in his denim jeans and a long-sleeved shirt.

   His polka-dot tie looks cool, too.

2. Kate looks great in that plaid silk skirt. Her cashmere turtleneck sweater goes with it really well, too.

   _____

   _____

3. Tiana's wearing dark blue skinny jeans – as usual – with a leather jacket. That look never goes out of fashion.

   _____

   _____

4. Ravi's light gray scarf goes perfectly with his suede jacket. Those fitted casual pants look great, too.

   _____

   _____

B Look at the pictures. Write descriptions of Angelo's and Risa's clothing.

1. Angelo _____

   _____

   _____

2. Risa _____

   _____

   _____

Lesson C / She has a big collection, then.

1 So, you must like . . .

Conversation strategies **Circle the response that best summarizes what A says.**

1. A I like music that's calm – music that helps
   me unwind after a crazy day.
   a. So, you have broad tastes, then.
   b. Uh-huh. You like music that's relaxing.

2. A I love Passion Pit. I've seen them in concert
   five times, and I have all their albums.
   a. So, you're a big fan.
   b. You like a lot of bands, then.

3. A I have a laptop, a smartphone, a tablet, and
   an e-reader.
   a. You don't know much about electronics.
   b. So, you have every gadget you need.

4. A I don't like the school cafeteria. They have
   the same things on the menu day after day.
   a. Yeah. I don't like it, either.
   b. Yeah. There's not much variety.

2 Summing it up

Conversation strategies **Complete the conversation with the sentences in the box.**

> ✓You have definite tastes, then.   You like songs that you know the lyrics to.
> You like clothes that you can wear every day. You want to understand what you're looking at.

Russ So anyway, you asked me what kind of music I like.
    Well, I like jazz, but I don't like blues. And I like rock,
    but I'm not really into pop. I guess I listen mostly to
    classical music, though not new stuff.

Liza *You have definite tastes, then.*

Russ Yeah. I guess. I just know what I like and what I don't.
    What about you?

Liza Well, I like music I can dance to – music that makes me feel good.
    I love it when I can sing along.

Russ I know what you mean. _____

Liza Exactly. I like music that puts me in a good mood.

Russ Yeah, I know what you're saying.

Liza It's the same with art. I like to be able to look at a picture and
    recognize what it is. Is it a flower or a car? Is it a man or a woman?
    You know what I mean?

Russ I know. _____

Liza That's right. I don't like art that's too weird.

Russ That's kind of how I feel about fashion. I like all the new
    fashions, but I'm not sure I'd ever wear them. Some styles
    are a little too weird for my taste, you know? They're just
    not practical.

Liza Right. _____

Russ Yes. I'm just conservative, I guess.

3 Now, what do you like?

Conversation strategies Add *Now* to the conversation in two appropriate places. Change the capital letters and add commas where necessary.

Avery I guess I'm pretty traditional, you know. I have conservative tastes in most things, like music and fashion.

Mike Really? I guess you don't listen to techno music, right?

Avery No way!

Mike _____ Are you the same about food, too?

Avery Actually, I like trying different foods. _____ I guess I'm not as conservative when it comes to eating.

Mike Interesting! _____ Have you tried sushi?

Avery Yes, I have. _____ And I love it!

4 Now, is there . . . ?

Conversation strategies Read Kay's comments about her likes and dislikes. Use the cues to complete each conversation with a summarizing response and a follow-up question with *Now*.

1. Kay I listen to all kinds of music – jazz, classical, hip-hop, rock.

    You (you / have / pretty broad tastes in music) *So, you have pretty broad tastes in music.*

    Kay Yeah, I guess I do!

    You (you / have a favorite) *Now, do you have a favorite?*

    Kay No, I pretty much like everything!

2. Kay Isn't this weather terrible? It's been over 90 degrees for at least eight days in a row! I can't stand it.

    You (you / not like / hot weather) _____

    Kay No, I don't like hot weather at all.

    You (you / like / cold weather) _____

    Kay Absolutely! I'm a skier, so I love cold weather.

3. Kay My car is really old, so I always worry that it's going to break down. I never know if it's going to start or not.

    You (it / be / pretty unreliable) _____

    Kay Yeah, it is. Maybe I need a new one.

    You (what kind of car / you / like) _____

    Kay I'm not really sure. Anything, if it's reliable.

1 Street fashion

Reading | **A** Read the interviews.

Which person is the most interested in fashion? _____
Who is the least interested? _____

How would you describe your style?

My style? It's casual and easy. I wear things that aren't too fussy – things that are comfortable and easy to wear. It's a little plain, but not too plain – I always wear a little color.

What does your style say about you?

My style says I'm easygoing. I like to look good, but I'm not going to spend a lot of time in front of the mirror. It says you should try to get to know me in a deeper way than just looking at the outside. There are other things more important than clothes.

How do you express yourself through the clothes you wear?

I don't, really. I don't spend a lot of time thinking about my clothes. I'd rather express myself in other ways, like talking to people or writing.

Sadie

How would you describe your style?

I wear casual but stylish things that don't stand out, or aren't too different. I like my clothes to be simple, but I usually take more of a risk with my shoes.

What does your style say about you?

It reflects my desire to be fashionable, but is not a demand for attention. For example, at parties I usually talk to one person at a time, rather than trying to be really outgoing. I'm more laid-back.

How do you express yourself through the clothes you wear?

My clothes are a way of showing the outside world what to expect. When I go out, people can guess that I'm relaxed and friendly. My clothes make me look approachable.

Carlos

How would you describe your style?

Unique. I mix lots of different styles together to make my individual style. Some days I'll wear a lace skirt with a plaid wool vest and tights in a cool pattern. And sometimes I'll put on a vintage hat to complete the look.

What does your style say about you?

My style says I'm unpredictable. I change from one day to the next. You can't put a particular label on me, like "She's preppy," or "She's classic," or "trendy," or whatever.

How do you express yourself through the clothes you wear?

It's fun to wear things that make people guess about you. People don't know who I am when they see my clothes, because I don't look just like everyone else. I like to be a little mysterious, to keep a few secrets about myself.

Michi

B Find the words below in the interviews and circle the best meaning.

1. fussy   a. simple   b. very detailed or decorated
2. stand out   a. look different   b. look the same
3. a desire   a. something you really want   b. something you don't want
4. approachable   a. easy to talk to   b. unfriendly or shy
5. unpredictable   a. conservative and average   b. strange and difficult to guess

C Read the questions. Check (✓) the names in the chart.

	Sadie	Carlos	Michi
1. Who likes to stand out in a crowd?	☐	☐	✓
2. Who likes to wear comfortable clothes?	☐	☐	☐
3. Who thinks their clothes shouldn't reveal their true personality?	☐	☐	☐
4. Who likes to change their look the most?	☐	☐	☐
5. Who likes to look nice, but not too different?	☐	☐	☐

2 Fashion tips

Writing **A** Read the fashion tips and add the appropriate punctuation: commas (,), dashes (–), or exclamation marks (!).

1. If you want to take care of your clothes you should wash them regularly dry them carefully and store them properly.

2. Choose clothes that make you feel good clothes that reflect your individual style.

3. Buy clothes that you can wear for more than one season that way you will get the most out of your new clothes.

4. Mix classic designs with trendier pieces wear simple black pants with a fun belt a trendy shirt and a classic jacket. You'll never be out of style.

B What is your fashion advice? Write three of your own fashion tips.

Unit 2 Progress chart

What can you do? Mark the boxes. ✓ = I can . . . 　 ? = I need to review how to . . .	To review, go back to these pages in the Student's Book.
Grammar ☐ make comparisons using *as . . . as* and *not as . . . as*.	12 and 13
☐ ask negative questions when I want someone to agree with me.	14
Vocabulary ☐ use at least 20 new words and expressions to talk about fashion.	12, 13, and 15
Conversation strategies ☐ show understanding by summarizing what someone says.	16
☐ use *Now* to introduce a follow-up question on a different aspect of a topic.	17
Writing ☐ use commas (,), dashes (–), and exclamation marks (!).	19

World cultures

Lesson A / Traditional things

1 Traditions

Grammar | **Complete the conversation with the simple present passive.**

Ken What's your favorite tradition from when you were a child?

Kerstin Hmm . . . let's see . . . I'd say Santa Lucia's Day.

Ken Santa Lucia's Day? I've never heard of it. Is it a Swedish festival?

Kerstin Yeah. It _'s celebrated___ (celebrate) on December thirteenth. It's the darkest time of winter, and Santa Lucia _____ (consider) to be the symbol of light. So, it reminds everyone that the days will get longer and sunnier after December.

Ken Oh, I see. So what do you do to celebrate?

Kerstin Well, in schools, for example, one girl _____ (choose) to be Santa Lucia. She wears a white dress, and a crown of candles _____ (place) on her head. Then the Santa Lucia song _____ (sing) by everyone. And in some families, the girl serves her parents breakfast in bed. That _____ (not do) in all homes, though.

Ken So, is there a special kind of food that _____ (eat), or anything?

Kerstin Yeah, they have these sweet buns that _____ (make) with spices. They _____ usually _____ (serve) with coffee – or juice for the kids.

Ken Huh. It sounds nice.

2 Did you know?

Grammar | **Rewrite each sentence using the simple present passive. Use *by* when the "doer" of the action is given.**

1. Some Native Americans carve totem poles out of wood.
   Totem poles are carved out of wood by some Native Americans.

2. They make the traditional Spanish dish, *paella*, with chicken, seafood, and saffron.
   _____

3. In Mexico, they celebrate the Day of the Dead on the first two days in November.
   _____

4. In Taiwan, parents give children red envelopes with money inside on New Year's Day.
   _____

So you want to know about Ireland . . .

Grammar | **Complete the web page with the verbs in the boxes. Use the simple present passive.**

○ ○ ○   About Ireland

ABOUT IRELAND

SPORTS
✓call   call   hold   play   use

The Irish love international sports like soccer and rugby, but they have their very own national sports, too. One traditional sport in Ireland _is called_ hurling. Sticks, or *hurleys*, _____ to hit a ball, a *sliotar*. Matches are usually 70 minutes long and _____ between two teams. Women play a similar sport, which _____ *camogie*. The final match _____ every September in Dublin.

MUSIC
call   learn   not use   perform   sing

Music is a strong tradition in Ireland. A typical musical event _____ a "session." Sessions _____ in pubs, clubs, and homes, where musicians and singers get together to play Irish music in an informal setting. Sheet music _____ at a traditional session because the tunes and songs _____ by heart. Some of the oldest songs _____ without musical accompaniment.

FOOD
boil   make   mash   mix   serve

One of Ireland's dishes, *colcannon*, _____ traditionally on Halloween. It _____ with potatoes and cabbage, which _____ in separate pots. The potatoes _____ until creamy, and then they _____ with the cabbage, leeks, milk, spices, and butter, and baked in a pan.

4 About you

Grammar | **Complete the questions with the verbs in parentheses. Then answer the questions with true information using the simple present passive.**

1. What sport _is considered_ (consider) a traditional sport in your country?
   Kite flying is considered a traditional sport in South Korea.

2. What handicrafts _____ typically _____ (make)?
   _____

3. What drinks _____ traditionally _____ (serve)?
   _____

4. What kinds of traditional games _____ (play)?
   _____

5. What special occasions _____ (celebrate)?
   _____

6. What traditional songs _____ (sing)?
   _____

1 Mind your manners!

Grammar and vocabulary | Use the words in the box to complete the sentences with either verb + *-ing* or *to* + verb.

1. Italy: It's customary _to kiss_ friends and family when you meet.
2. South Korea: _____ your bare feet to elderly people is disrespectful.
3. Indonesia: _____ and drinking before you are asked to by your host is rude.
4. The U.S.A.: It's impolite _____ at a bus stop or in a bank, for example.
5. Mexico: _____ is the normal way to greet people in a business situation.
6. Japan: It's important _____ your shoes before you enter someone's home.
7. Saudi Arabia: _____ in public is a sign of friendship.
8. Germany: If you're sitting, it's polite _____ when greeting people and shaking their hands.

cut in line
eat
hold hands
✓ kiss
shake hands
show
stand up
take off

2 Manners dos and don'ts

Grammar and vocabulary | Look at the pictures and complete the sentences.

1. In the United States, you should try _to keep_ your voice down in a library.

2. In Japan, _____ is a way of showing respect.

3. _____ an argument in public in Vietnam is considered bad manners.

4. _____ around barefoot in Belize is an acceptable custom.

5. It's acceptable not _____ waiters in Australia, unless you're at a very fancy restaurant.

6. It's bad manners in Indonesia _____ at someone with your finger.

3 Good manners

Grammar | Complete the sentences with the correct form of the verbs. Then check (✓) the sentences that are true in your country. Circle the six most important ones.

GOOD MANNERS CHECKLIST

1. _____ You can offend people by _reaching_ (reach) across a table for something.
2. _____ It's polite _____ (say) hello to your teacher when you arrive in class.
3. _____ _____ (eat) on the subway is considered rude.
4. _____ _____ (be) five minutes late for a meeting is acceptable.
5. _____ It's considered rude _____ (shout) at someone.
6. _____ It's not acceptable _____ (go) to a party uninvited.
7. _____ People are expected _____ (be) on time for medical and dental appointments.
8. _____ Be careful not _____ (leave) work without _____ (say) good night to your co-workers.
9. _____ _____ (give) money for a wedding gift is common.
10. _____ _____ (ask) about someone's age might be offensive.
11. _____ When a train stops, it's better _____ (wait) for people to get off before _____ (get) on yourself.
12. _____ It's bad manners _____ (talk) loudly on a cell phone in public places.

4 About you

Grammar | Rewrite the sentences using *not* to give them an opposite meaning. Then check (✓) the sentences that are true in your country.

1. _____ It's OK to point at people in public places.
   _____ _It's not OK to point at people in public places._

2. _____ It's customary to walk in someone's house without taking off your shoes.
   _____ _____

3. _____ Try to stand close to people you're talking to.
   _____ _____

4. _____ Opening a gift in front of the person who gave it to you is considered rude.
   _____ _____

5. _____ You can annoy people by saying you're sorry if you bump into them.
   _____ _____

6. _____ It's customary to tip hairstylists.
   _____ _____

7. _____ Being early for a party is considered polite.
   _____ _____

8. _____ Talking on a cell phone in a public place is acceptable.
   _____ _____

Lesson C / To be honest, . . .

1 I really like it.

Conversation strategies Rewrite each response using the best expression to make the response sound more direct.

1. A Do you like your new dorm?
   B Yeah. I like it.
   ((really)/ sort of) *I really like it.*

2. A What's your new roommate like?
   B Well, I don't really like her.
   (to be honest / I guess) _____

3. A Do you miss anything about your old school?
   B No. I hated my old school.
   (absolutely / a little bit) _____

4. A Do you ever think about studying abroad?
   B Yes! I would like to do that.
   (kind of / definitely) _____

5. A If you moved away, would you miss your family?
   B Oh, I'd miss my family, especially my brother.
   (in a way / certainly) _____

2 About you 1

Conversation strategies Rewrite the sentences so that they are true for you. Use different expressions from the box. Add more information.

| absolutely | certainly | honestly | really | to tell you the truth |
| actually | definitely | in fact | to be honest | |

1. I love learning about new cultures.
   I really love learning about new cultures. I'd absolutely love to go to Kenya.

2. I don't think it would be exciting to live in a new city.
   _____

3. I'd miss home cooking if I lived in another country.
   _____

4. I'd hate to live with a roommate. I'd prefer to live by myself.
   _____

5. I'd like to live all over the world. I can't imagine living in just one place.
   _____

6. I'm sure I'd get homesick if I lived a long way from home.
   _____

3 Of course . . .

Conversation
strategies Use *of course* twice in each conversation where it is appropriate and not rude. Leave one blank in each conversation empty. Add commas where necessary.

1. **Bruno** I hear you decided to study abroad next year. Where are you going?

   Kara _____ I'm going to Mexico!

   Bruno You must be so excited! I know I would be.

   Kara Yeah, I'm definitely excited, but I'm really nervous, too.

   Bruno Just think about all the cool experiences you'll have.

   Kara Yeah, I know. But I'm going to miss you _____ !
   I mean, who am I going to talk to when I have a problem?

   Bruno Well, *me* _____ . We can always chat over the Internet!

   Kara Right. . . . I forgot about that!

2. **Yumi** Hi, Brad. How was your business trip?

   Brad To tell you the truth, it was awful. The day I left, the
   traffic was really bad, so I got to the airport late.
   And _____ I missed my flight.

   Yumi So, you were probably late for the sales meeting, then?

   Brad Yeah _____ . Then, because I was so stressed
   out, I forgot to give Mr. Yamamoto my business card.

   Yumi I'm sure he understood.

   Brad Yeah, and I apologized right away _____ .

   Yumi So, it doesn't sound like your trip was that bad.

4 About you 2

Conversation
strategies **Answer the questions directly and confidently with true information.
Then add a follow-up sentence with *of course*.**

1. Would you jump at the chance to study in another country?
   I'd absolutely jump at the chance to study in another country.
   Of course, I'd have to learn the language first.

2. What would you miss about your country if you lived abroad?
   _____
   _____

3. If you had the opportunity to live someplace else, where would it be?
   _____
   _____

4. What would be the first thing you'd do after moving to a new city?
   _____
   _____

1 Proverbs for everyday living

Reading | **A Read the article. Which sentence best states the writer's attitude toward proverbs?**

1. Proverbs are fun but not meaningful.
2. Proverbs about love are truer than proverbs about sports or money.
3. Proverbs can help and guide us in different life situations.
4. Proverbs are never true.

Timeless wisdom

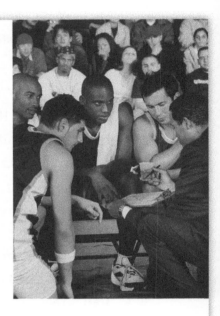

No matter what problem we have or what issue we are discussing, there always seems to be a memorable proverb that neatly sums up the situation, provides some wisdom, or simply makes us feel better. We find a selection that will inspire us, make us wiser, and console us through hard times. Sports, money, and love are just three of the areas that have inspired a number of well-used proverbs.

SPORTS   There are probably few coaches who haven't called on a proverb or two to motivate their players. Players who aren't working to their full potential might benefit from hearing "no pain, no gain" and understand that increasing performance on the field requires more hard work and effort. During intense parts of a game, a coach might yell, "No guts, no glory!" to push his or her players into scoring a goal. "There is no *I* in *team*" encourages teamwork and reminds players that not being the "star" of the team might be hard, but it could mean a stronger winning team.

MONEY   The proverb "A fool and his money are soon parted" describes a person who has money but squanders it on poor choices. A person who doesn't understand that it takes hard work to make money might benefit from the proverb "Money doesn't grow on trees." If it did, it would be easy to find and everyone would have an abundance of it. On the other hand, it's important to remember that money isn't always the answer to our problems. Sometimes we have to remind ourselves that "the best things in life are free" – for example, good health, family, and friends.

LOVE   The proverb "Love is blind" means that if you are in love with someone, you overlook all their negative points. It's often said when you don't approve of a friend's partner; it offers an explanation for what you see as a poor choice. Then, when relationships go through sad or emotional times, the proverb "Love conquers all" reminds us that it's wise to approach these problems with love because they will be easier to handle. Love will get you through most difficult situations.

B Find these words and phrases in the article. Match them with their definitions.

1. sums up ___f___
2. console _____
3. potential _____
4. squander _____
5. abundance _____
6. conquers _____

a. waste
b. ability
c. an amount that is more than enough
d. defeats, beats
e. give comfort or sympathy to
✓f. explains without detail

2 If at first you don't succeed, . . .

Writing **A** Read about an athlete's favorite proverb. Fill in the blanks with the expressions in the box.

I like this proverb because it means that it's often said that one of my favorite proverbs is

As a college wrestler, I compete with some of the toughest and most disciplined athletes. _____ "fall seven times, stand up eight." To me, _____ you should never give up on your goals and dreams no matter how hard practice is every day or how many important matches you lose. _____ athletes can't win unless they believe in themselves. _____ it reminds me that no matter how many times I fail, if I don't stand up after my failure, I'll never succeed.

B Describe a proverb that you use for motivation in your life. Use the expressions above.

Unit 3 Progress chart

What can you do? Mark the boxes. ✓ = I can . . . ? = I need to review how to . . .	To review, go back to these pages in the Student's Book.
Grammar ☐ use the simple present passive to talk about cultural traditions.	22 and 23
☐ use verb + -ing as a subject, and as an object of a preposition.	24 and 25
☐ use to + verb after It's.	24 and 25
Vocabulary ☐ use at least 10 expressions to talk about different customs and manners.	24 and 25
Conversation strategies ☐ use expressions like to be honest to sound more direct.	26
☐ use of course to give information that is not surprising or to agree.	27
Writing ☐ use expressions like It means . . . to talk about culture or proverbs.	29

25

1 What are you supposed to do?

Grammar and vocabulary | Look at the pictures. Complete the sentences with *be supposed to* and an appropriate verb. Use negatives where necessary.

1. You *'re not supposed to park* on the street.
   You *'re supposed to park* in the parking lot.

2. They _____ shoes inside.
   They _____ their shoes.

3. She _____ at the dentist.
   She _____ home.

4. He _____ his room.
   He _____ on the phone.

2 It was supposed to be a nice weekend.

Grammar | Complete the email with the correct form of *be supposed to* or *was / were going to*. Sometimes more than one answer is possible.

New Message

Hey Jane,

    I had a terrible weekend. On Saturday morning, I _was going to / was supposed to_ go running with a friend because the weather _____ be nice. But it rained, and she didn't come. She emailed me and wrote, "I _____ come, but when I saw the weather, I decided to stay in bed. Sorry."

    Then my parents came over to my apartment – they were two hours early. They _____ come at 1:00, but they came at 11:00. The apartment was a complete mess! They took me to that new Mexican place on Oak Street. Have you been there? It _____ be really good. But it was completely booked – I didn't realize that you _____ make reservations.

    So then we tried an Italian place across the street. That was nice, but I didn't know my pasta dish had shrimp in it. I'm allergic to shrimp, and I _____ avoid it. So I got sick. Now here's the worst part. I _____ go to a party on Saturday night, but I couldn't because I still felt sick. I sure hope next weekend will be better.

Take care!
Allie

---

3 I was supposed to . . .

Grammar | **Complete the conversation with the correct form of *be supposed to* or *was / were going to*. Sometimes more than one correct answer is possible.**

Christy   Hi, Zach. Are you going to Isabelle's party tonight?

Zach   Yeah, I am, actually. I *was supposed to meet / was going to meet*
(meet) my parents for dinner, but they canceled. So, now I can go.

Christy   Great! I _____ (pick up) Sanjay at 7:00.
Do you need a ride?

Zach   Sure, thanks. Now, I can't remember. . . . _____
we _____ (bring) anything like food or drinks?

Christy   No, only if you want to. I _____
(not / make) anything, but maybe I will if I have time.

Zach   You should make those chocolate chip cookies you brought
to the last party. They were awesome.

Christy   Yeah, they are pretty good. But they have nuts in them.
Isabelle _____ (not / eat) nuts
because she's allergic to them.

Zach   Right. Maybe you should just make a chocolate cake or something.

Christy   Good idea. Oh, and don't forget to bring your bathing suit and a towel.
The weather _____ (be) great tonight, and Isabelle's
pool is beautiful.

Zach   Sounds like a plan to me!

4 About you

Grammar | **Answer the questions with your own information. Use *be supposed to* or *was / were going to*. Use negatives and contractions where necessary.**

1. Is there anything you have to do to prepare for your English class?
   For our next class, we're supposed to bring in some photos.

2. What's the weather forecast for tomorrow?
   _____

3. What do you have to do tomorrow?
   _____

4. What plans do you have for this week?
   _____

5. What appointment or plans did you cancel last month?
   _____

6. What exciting future plans do you have?
   _____

1 Get away with . . .

Vocabulary | **A** Complete the sentences with the appropriate *get* expression.

1. In some companies, you can <u>g e t a w a y w i t h</u> wearing casual clothes to work. In my company, you have to dress more formally.

2. I'm so busy at work that I don't have time to answer all my emails right away, but I always ____ ____ ____ ____ ____ ____ ____ ____ ____ ____ ____ them eventually.

3. I have a business trip next week, but I'm going to try to ____ ____ ____ ____ ____ ____ ____ ____ it. I'm tired of traveling so much.

4. Someone else got the promotion I wanted at work. I'm upset, but I'll ____ ____ ____ ____ ____ ____ ____ it soon.

5. My friend's always late for work. I just don't ____ ____ ____ ____ ____! How does he keep his job?

6. My office doesn't have windows. It's depressing. I don't think I'll ever ____ ____ ____ ____ ____ ____ ____ ____ ____ not having sunlight.

7. During the summer, my company has new hours – we ____ ____ ____ ____ ____ ____ work at noon on Fridays!

8. My boss never returns my phone calls. I ____ ____ ____ ____ ____ ____ ____ ____ ____ ____ ____ ____ ____ that he's avoiding me.

9. Tonight there's a company party so new employees can ____ ____ ____ ____ ____ ____ ____ ____ ____ everyone. I really hope to ____ ____ ____ ____ ____ ____ ____ early. I hate these functions. But, the good food should help me ____ ____ ____ ____ ____ ____ ____ ____ ____ it OK.

10. I have a meeting in ten minutes! I really have to ____ ____ ____ ____ ____ ____ ____ ____ .

B Complete the conversations with some of the *get* expressions from part A.

1. A Oh, I can't believe it's already 8:30! I'd better <u>get going</u> if I want to catch the 9:00 train.

   B Yeah, I don't think you can _____ being late again.

   A I know, but it's so hard to get up in the morning. . . .

   B I don't _____ . How can you complain? You _____ work so early. I'd love your job!

2. A What time do you think you'll finish work tonight? Do you think you can _____ from work a little early?

   B Sure, I have a late meeting, but I can probably _____ it. Why? I _____ you have something planned. . . .

   A Did you _____ reading yesterday's restaurant review?

   B Yeah, for that amazing restaurant with the six-month waiting list?

   A Well, we're going tonight!

2 I get the feeling . . .

Grammar and vocabulary | **Complete the anecdotes. Put the words in order and use the correct form of the verbs.**

1. Melanie was very superstitious. She couldn't _get over her fear_
   (over / her fear / get) of seeing black cats. She thought they were so
   unlucky. Now she can't _____
   (get / a day / through) without running into one.

2. Gary was supposed to meet Tracy at the movies, but he really wanted to
   _____ (get / of / go / out) with her. He called Tracy and said
   he couldn't _____ (work / off / get) early on Friday night.
   Instead, Gary made arrangements to go to the movies with Marissa.
   He really thought he could _____ (it / away / get / with).
   But he didn't – as he found out when he ran into Tracy at the
   movie theater!

3. John didn't _____ (pay / around / to / get) his
   electricity bill. He thought he could _____
   (get / with / away / make) the payment a few days late. Now he has
   to _____ (to / used / eat / get) dinner in the dark!

3 About you

Grammar and vocabulary | **Answer the questions with true information.**

1. What haven't you gotten around to doing this week?
   I haven't gotten around to cleaning my room.

2. Have you bought anything new that took time to get used to?
   _____

3. What's a chore you always try to get out of doing?
   _____

4. What events do you find it hard to get through?
   _____

5. What time do you get off work?
   _____

6. How long did it take you to get over your last cold?
   _____

1 So, you're throwing a party?

Conversation strategies

A Unscramble these statement questions.

1. right / you, / is / It ?
   It is you, right?

2. teenagers, / huh / So / teach / you ?
   _____

3. them / haven't / So / told / you / yet ?
   _____

4. that software company, / working / still / You're / at / right ?
   _____

5. know / then / here, / don't / So / they / you're ?
   _____

6. huh / about / didn't / You / hear / that, ?
   _____

B Complete the conversation with the statement questions from part A.

Eva   Oh, my gosh. Dan? I haven't seen you in ages!

Dan   Eva? *It is you, right?* _____ You look great!
How are you?

Eva   Oh, I'm fine. Thanks. So, what are you up to?
_____

Dan   Cyber-trex? Actually, no, not anymore. They went out of
business. _____

Eva   No, I didn't. I'm sorry.

Dan   Oh, it's OK. I'm at Micro-com now. I like it a lot better.
So, what's up with you?

Eva   Um, I teach history at the local high school.

Dan   Wow! _____ What's that like?

Eva   It's really good. The students are great. Anyway, what brings you back here?

Dan   Well, I'm in town to throw my parents a surprise party for their
40th wedding anniversary.

Eva   _____

Dan   No, not yet! In fact, my brother and sister don't even know I'm here.

Eva   _____ About the party, I mean.

Dan   No, I couldn't. They can't keep a secret to save their lives!

2 So, you're having a birthday party?

Conversation
strategies | **Find three more places where you can use *so* in the conversation. Change the capital letters and add commas where necessary. Then write which meaning of *so* you are using: 1 = to start a topic with a question; 2 = to check your understanding; 3 = to pause or let the other person draw a conclusion; 4 = to close a topic.**

Rita   <u>So,</u> *<s>Y</s>*ou're having a birthday party this year?   <u>1</u>

Craig   I don't know. ____ My birthday is going to fall right in   ____
the middle of final exams.

Rita   ____ You think people won't come if they're studying?   ____

Craig   Yeah, I mean, these are important exams, _____ . . .   ____
you know, everyone is working hard to get good grades.

Rita   ____ Well, maybe you could wait until after the   ____
exams are over.

Craig   Yeah, I guess I could.

Rita   Then you can have a double celebration: for your   ____
birthday *and* the end of exams. ____

Craig   That's a good idea.

Rita   ____ Don't forget to invite me!   ____

Craig   I won't!

3 A late night

Conversation
strategies | **Complete the conversation with the sentences in the box.**

> So you're not too tired to go out tonight?   You're going out again tonight?
> You didn't do anything?   ✓You stayed out pretty late, huh?
> You had a good time, right?

Keith   Oh, . . . I'm so tired. That was a long night last night.

Phil   *You stayed out pretty late, huh?* ____

Keith   Yeah, until about 2:30 in the morning. But it was fun.

Phil   _____

Keith   Oh, definitely. The band was great – just awesome.
So, anyway, what about you? Did you go out?

Phil   No. . . . I just stayed home. That's all.

Keith   _____

Phil   No. I was just here all night.

Keith   Too bad. Do you want to come out tonight? Are you doing anything?

Phil   I don't have any plans yet. _____

Keith   Well, I was thinking about it. But I don't want to be out too late.

Phil   _____

Keith   Too tired to go out? No way! I'll be fine later.

Phil   Sounds good to me.

1 First impressions

Reading | **A** Read the article. Then add the correct heading to each section.

> Be fearless.   Pay attention to your body language.   Use your ears.
> Maintain eye contact.   ✓ Smile!

SOCIALIZING 101

Whether you are an extrovert or an introvert, one thing is certain: Almost everyone experiences some degree of stress when it comes to being sociable in new situations. It doesn't matter if you're starting a new job, going back to school, or if you're waiting in line at a coffee shop. The next time you're out and about, try one of these tips to help you become better at socializing.

_____ *Smile!* _____ One of the easiest and most effective ways to be more sociable is to smile. Remember: You're supposed to be having fun. When you strike up a conversation, a warm smile will make you seem more approachable and friendly. Don't be surprised when the person you start a conversation with reciprocates with an equally warm smile!

_____ Once you've started a conversation, make sure you keep your eyes focused on the person you're talking to. There's nothing more off-putting than talking to someone whose eyes are wandering around the room rather than paying attention to the conversation. Not every conversation is interesting, but there's no reason to be rude.

_____ When you cross your arms in front of you while standing or you cross your legs while sitting, you are literally keeping people at a distance. Try to keep an open, relaxed position, and people will feel more comfortable approaching you.

_____ Having a conversation is a two-way street. Ask engaging questions, and then really listen to what your conversation partner says. Who knows? You may discover you have common musical interests, or you might even get a recommendation for a great restaurant. You'll never know if you don't listen closely.

_____ Don't stand around waiting for someone to start talking with you. Get over your fear and be the person who initiates conversations. Most people are open to having a warm, meaningful conversation, especially when they are out in a social situation. Walking up to a stranger may seem daunting at first, but once you've done it a few times, it will seem natural and maybe even fun!

B Find these words and expressions in the article. Match them with their meanings.

1. reciprocate __e__
2. off-putting ____
3. wandering ____
4. literally ____
5. engaging ____
6. initiate ____
7. daunting ____

a. interesting
b. actually
c. slightly frightening
d. annoying or unpleasant
✓e. behave in the same way
f. going around with no clear purpose
g. start, cause something to begin

C Read the article again. Check (✓) the statements that the writer of the article would agree with. Cross (✗) the ones that the writer wouldn't agree with.

1. __✗__ There's no reason to be nervous when you socialize.
2. __✓__ Socializing is easier when you smile.
3. _____ People are supposed to enjoy socializing.
4. _____ It's not rude to look around the room when you're talking to someone.
5. _____ Crossing your arms is a good idea because it helps you feel comfortable.
6. _____ Socializing is more difficult when you only listen.
7. _____ Conversations with strangers can lead to all kinds of new possibilities.
8. _____ You can get used to socializing, and then it will be easier.

2 As an introvert

Writing **A** Read the short article about meeting new people. Replace each underlined *as* with *because, being,* or *while*.

> As an introvert, I have a hard time meeting new people. I usually don't like to go to parties where there are lots of people I don't know.
> When I travel, though, I am less shy. I find I can talk to people as I wait to get on a plane or train. Maybe I feel more comfortable as I'm away from home and I can be who I want to be. But when I get back home, I'm shy again!

B Write a short article about how you meet new people.

Unit 4 Progress chart

What can you do? Mark the boxes. ✓ = I can . . . ? = I need to review how to . . .	To review, go back to these pages in the Student's Book.
Grammar	
use *be supposed to* to say what should happen.	34 and 35
use *be supposed to* to talk about things I should do.	34 and 35
use *was / were supposed to* and *was / were going to* for things that didn't happen.	34 and 35
use inseparable phrasal verbs with and without prepositions.	36 and 37
Vocabulary	
use at least 10 new expressions with *get*.	36 and 37
Conversation strategies	
use statement questions to check understanding.	38
use *so* to start or close topics, pause, or check understanding.	39
Writing	
use three different meanings of *as*.	41

Law and order

1 Something ought to be done.

Grammar | Rewrite the sentences in the passive form, starting with the words given.

1. They must change the law. The law _must be changed_ .
2. They should ban fireworks. Fireworks _____ .
3. They ought to fine people who litter. People who litter _____ .
4. They shouldn't allow smoking on the street. Smoking _____ on the street.
5. They could encourage healthy eating in schools. Healthy eating _____ in schools.
6. They have to do something about violent movies. Something _____ about violent movies.

2 What's your opinion?

Grammar and vocabulary | **A** Circle the correct words to complete the opinions.

1. People should not be (encouraged)/ **changed** / **passed** to keep dangerous pets like snakes and spiders.
2. Cell phones shouldn't be **fined** / **allowed** / **given** in museums.
3. People who litter should be **encouraged** / **allowed** / **fined** at least $100 for each item they drop.
4. People should be **given** / **made** / **changed** to vote.
5. Laws have to be **passed** / **arrested** / **done** to ban smoking in all public places.
6. Young people ought to be **banned** / **made** / **given** a driving test every year until they are 21.
7. Smoking on city streets could easily be **made** / **passed** / **banned**.
8. People should be **arrested** / **made** / **changed** for not carrying an ID.

B Do you agree or disagree with the opinions in part A? Answer with your own opinions.

1. _I agree completely. I don't think people should be allowed to keep dangerous pets at all._
2. _____
3. _____
4. _____
5. _____
6. _____
7. _____
8. _____

3 What should be done?

Grammar | **Read the situations and complete the comments. Use the passive of the verbs given.**

1. A woman is facing a large fine because her neighbor complained to the police about her messy yard. The angry woman then dumped her garbage in the neighbor's yard.

   A I think the fine is absolutely right. You shouldn't _be allowed_ (allow) to have a messy yard.

   B I don't agree. She shouldn't _____ (fine). It's her own property, and she should be able to do what she wants.

   C The woman should _____ (arrest) for dumping garbage in her neighbor's yard!

2. A motorcycle rider was arrested by the police for refusing to wear a helmet. The motorcyclist said that he couldn't wear the helmet because of his traditional headdress.

   A I agree with the motorcyclist. He shouldn't _____ (make) to wear a helmet.

   B People shouldn't _____ (arrest) for not wearing a helmet. It's their choice.

   C Well, everyone has to obey the law. People shouldn't _____ (treat) differently.

3. A foreign exchange student who failed to show his ID was given a warning after a local storeowner called the police. In an unrelated incident, a young woman riding her bike to work was fined for failing to carry her ID.

   A I didn't know you could _____ (fine) for not carrying an ID.

   B It's a new law, but I think it ought to _____ (change).

   C I wonder why the police stopped the woman. People shouldn't _____ (stop) for no reason.

4 About you

Grammar | **Read the situations and give your own opinion. Use passive modal verbs.**

1. A 13-year-old boy sneaks into an R-rated movie. What ought to be done?
   He ought to be made to tell his parents.

2. A man throws a soda can out of his car window. Should he be arrested or fined?
   _____

3. A 16-year-old student wants a part-time job. Should she be encouraged to get one?
   _____

4. A 15-year-old girl applies for a credit card. Should she be given one?
   _____

5. A 12-year-old boy spends three hours a day online. Should he be given a time limit?
   _____

6. An 85-year-old man was in six minor car accidents this year. Should he be allowed to drive?
   _____

1 What's the crime?

Vocabulary Match the words in Column A with the words in Column B to make expressions for crimes and punishments. Write the expressions under the appropriate heading in the chart.

Column A
put
armed
lose
break into
kill
take someone
send
minor
clean up
go to

Column B
a house
offense
on probation
robbery
graffiti
to prison
captive
jail
your license
someone

Crime	Punishment
	put on probation

2 News flash

Vocabulary Complete the news flashes with the words in the box.

jaywalker	penalties	sentence	stealing
kidnapper	robbers	✓ shoplifters	vandals

1. A TV actress was caught stealing in a designer store. The manager said ___shoplifters___ will be punished even if they're famous.

2. The number of robberies has declined. Police say more _____ are getting caught.

3. A murderer who was convicted of killing his boss receives a _____ of life in prison.

4. Three _____ were caught on camera spray-painting graffiti on office buildings. All three were put on probation for two years.

5. _____ for a first-time speeding offense now include a $500 fine.

6. A _____ was arrested after crossing in the middle of a busy street.

7. A _____ demands $10,000,000 after taking a politician's daughter from her home.

8. A teen was arrested for _____ money from a neighbor's house. Police say the 17-year-old broke into the neighbor's house while she was at work.

3 In the news

Grammar | Imagine you are telling a friend about the excerpts from the newspaper below. Rewrite each sentence in the passive. Change the underlined verbs to the *get* passive, or use the *be* passive with *should*. Make any other necessary changes.

> **1** Police <u>arrested</u> three teenagers yesterday for stealing a car.   **2** The officers <u>caught</u> them joyriding along a busy street.   **3** The owner of the car thinks they should <u>fine</u> the teens.

1. " *Three teenagers got arrested yesterday for stealing a car.* "

2. "_____"

3. "_____"

> **4** Fans think a TV network should <u>make</u> reality-TV star Lulu Maxwell give a public apology.   **5** The county court <u>fined</u> Maxwell $500 and <u>put</u> her on probation for six months.   **6** Store detectives <u>caught</u> her shoplifting in a department store downtown in March of this year.

4. "_____"

5. "_____"

6. "_____"

> **7** Car owners <u>caught</u> a man writing graffiti on their cars last Wednesday. **8** The judge <u>convicted</u> Jim Hillman yesterday of vandalism.   **9** The owners of the cars believe they should <u>make</u> Hillman pay for the damage done to their vehicles.

7. "_____"

8. "_____"

9. "_____"

4 About you

Grammar | Answer the questions with true information. Use the *get* passive.

1. What happens if you get caught shoplifting in your country?
   *You get fined and perhaps put in jail.*_____

2. What's the punishment for writing graffiti on a public building?

   _____

3. What's the punishment for murder?

   _____

4. What happens if you jaywalk?

   _____

5. What happens if you get caught speeding too many times?

   _____

1 Basically, I don't think . . .

Conversation strategies Choose the best expressions to complete the conversation.

Roy   Did you know that Sam got caught cheating on the test?

Helen   Yeah, it's about time. He cheats on all his tests.
I wonder what the teacher's going to do about it.

Roy   I don't know. What do you think they should do?

Helen   Hmm. Well, **another thing is** / (**basically,**) I don't think
he should get away with it.

Roy   Well, no, I guess not.

Helen   I mean, **for a couple of reasons** / **the point is**. First of all, it's
not fair to the other students, and **number one** / **second of all**, it doesn't help the
person who cheats. I mean, **the thing is** / **another thing is**, I don't think Sam's really learning.

Roy   I know what you mean.

Helen   And **for two reasons** / **another thing is**, if they don't punish him, it might make other students
think they can cheat, too.

Roy   Yeah. I guess you're right.

2 I mean, the thing is, . . .

Conversation strategies **A** Read what Carl has to say about carrying ID cards. Number the lines in the
correct order from 1 to 7.

_____ I mean, ID cards make things easier for two reasons.

_1_ What do I think about having to carry an ID card?

_____ And then, secondly, if you have an accident or something, people can find out
who you are right away.

_____ And finally . . . um, I guess I just don't mind. You have nothing to be afraid of
if you have nothing to hide. Don't you think?

_____ First, they help the police identify criminals more easily.

_____ Well, I guess basically, I'm in favor of carrying them.

_____ And another thing is, people who work in movie theaters and other places can
easily check who is old enough to go in and stuff.

B What do you think about carrying an ID card? Write four sentences. Use words
and expressions from part A and Exercise 1 to organize your ideas.

_____

_____

_____

_____

_____

3 That's true, but . . .

Conversation strategies **Match Diego's opinions with his friends' responses. There is one extra response.**

1. I don't think jaywalking should be a crime. I mean, if I'm in a hurry, I should be able to cross the street wherever I want to! _____

2. I think couples that are getting married should be made to take marriage classes before they actually get married. You know, to help lower divorce rates. _____

3. I think it's the parents' responsibility to make sure their kids know right from wrong. I mean, if the kids do something wrong, their parents should be punished, too. _____

4. You know, there are just too many laws for everything! The thing is, most people are sensible enough not to need all these laws. _____

a. You've got a point there, but don't you think that parents with kids that are always in trouble should be helped, not punished?

b. Well, you've got a point, but society would be a big mess without them! I think people actually need them.

c. That's true – maybe it shouldn't be a crime – but you still need to be careful, especially if you're in a hurry.

d. That's true, but on the other hand, kids are kids, and we have to treat them all the same.

e. I never really thought of it that way. It's not such a bad idea, but I'm not sure that taking classes would help.

4 The point is, . . .

Conversation strategies **Complete the conversation with the words and expressions in the box.**

another thing is	I never thought of it that way	number two	there are two reasons
basically	number one	✓ their point is	you've got a point

Pam　Did you hear they won't let students bring snacks to class anymore? Some teachers complained that students spend too much time eating when they should be taking notes. I guess _their point is_ , students aren't paying enough attention.

Roger　I don't think that's right. I mean, _____ , you should be allowed to bring a snack.

Pam　Why do you think that?

Roger　Well, I mean, . . . _____ . I guess, _____ , you don't always have enough time between classes to get something to eat. And _____ , some classes are three hours long! You really need to eat just to stay awake! And, _____ , the teachers sometimes have drinks and things while they're teaching.

Pam　Hmm. . . . _____ there, but in some classes, students just leave the garbage from their snacks and drinks all over the desks. It's really disgusting.

Roger　Yeah, that's true. I must admit, . . . _____ .

1 Dumb criminals

Reading **A** Read the article below. Then match the stories with the pictures.

Dumb Criminals

We all know that crime is serious and that criminals should be punished. However, it's hard not to smile when you hear about criminals like the ones in these stories, who made some dumb mistakes.

1. A thief stole 27 shoes from a store, without realizing that they were all right-footed. He wasn't arrested, but he certainly didn't get what he wanted.

2. A burglar was caught sleeping in an armchair of the house he was burglarizing when the owners came home.

3. Robbers stole $1,221 of electronics from a store. All the goods were faulty items returned by customers.

4. A man stole a police car in order to get to work. He was discovered when he stopped to help someone on the side of the road who flagged him down for help.

5. A woman walked into a fast-food restaurant early one morning and demanded money. The clerk said he couldn't open the cash drawer without a food order. When the woman grudgingly ordered onion rings, the clerk said they weren't available for breakfast. The woman became frustrated and walked out.

6. A man walked into a convenience store and asked for change, putting a twenty-dollar bill on the counter. When the cashier opened the drawer, the man demanded all the money in it. Then he ran out, leaving his twenty on the counter. The cashier reported that the man fled with about $17 in cash.

B Answer the questions about the criminals above.

Criminal 1: What didn't he notice? *He didn't notice all the shoes were right-footed.*

Criminal 2: Why was he caught? _____

Criminal 3: Why weren't these robbers happy? _____

Criminal 4: What was his mistake? _____

Criminal 5: What did she need to order? _____

Criminal 6: How much did his crime cost him? _____

2 A bad landing . . .

Writing **A** Read the police report. Add *because*, *since*, or *as*. Sometimes more than one answer is possible.

> ### POLICE REPORT
>
> A woman was arrested for trying to rob a convenience store. _____ she didn't
> know the store was open 24 hours a day, she broke in through the roof. Unfortunately for
> her, she fell through the roof and landed on top of a coffee machine. A police officer was
> inside the store, and he didn't have to go far to make the arrest _____ he was
> right there getting his coffee! _____ the woman was slightly injured, she went to
> the hospital first before going to jail. She was treated for minor cuts and coffee burns.

B Write a short story or article about something funny that has happened to you.
Use *because*, *since*, or *as* to give reasons for the events.

Unit 5 Progress chart

What can you do? Mark the boxes. ✓ = I can . . . ? = I need to review how to . . .	To review, go back to these pages in the Student's Book.
Grammar ☐ use the passive of modal verbs.	44 and 45
☐ use the *get* passive.	46 and 47
Vocabulary ☐ use at least 25 expressions to talk about rules, regulations, crimes, and punishments.	44, 45, 46, and 47
Conversation strategies ☐ organize what I say with expressions like *First of all*, etc.	48
☐ use expressions like *That's a good point* to show someone else has a valid argument.	49
Writing ☐ give reasons using *because*, *since*, and *as*.	51

Strange events

Lesson A / Coincidences

1 My strange experiences

Vocabulary | Complete Ava's blog with the words and expressions in the box.

coincidences	out of the blue	sticks in my mind	✓UFO
déjà vu	ran into	telepathy	unexpectedly

Ava's Blog

Nothing really strange has ever happened to me. I've never seen a ___*UFO*___ . And I don't believe in _____ – you know, that you can tell what someone else is thinking. I've never even had that strange feeling of _____ , like I've been someplace before. The only weird thing that _____ is meeting someone with the same birthday as mine. But that's about it.

However, I absolutely believe strange _____ happen all the time. In fact, last week, I called a friend completely _____ at the same time she was calling me. That was pretty funny. A couple of years ago, I _____ that same friend at a restaurant while I was on vacation – completely _____ . Oh, and another time, I was on the Internet and typed in the wrong URL. I found a website about my old high school science teacher. He'd invented a new type of vacuum cleaner and had become a millionaire! Cool, huh?

2 What a coincidence!

Grammar and vocabulary | Complete the story. Use the simple past or the past perfect. Sometimes more than one answer is possible.

One night about a year ago, I went out with some friends. I didn't really want to go out because I _*had broken up*_ (break up) with my girlfriend a week or so earlier. Anyway, I met this great girl, and we _____ (start) talking. We had a great time and danced all night. So, we _____ (decide) to meet the next day, and to make a long story short, we started dating.

We _____ (date) for about four months when she _____ (invite) me to a party at her apartment. I was looking at the pictures of her college friends around her apartment, and I _____ (notice) that my cousin Ciara from Chicago was in one of her photos. It turns out that my girlfriend and my cousin _____ (be) roommates for over three years in college, but they _____ (not see) each other for about a year. What a coincidence!

3 A mystery ride

Grammar and vocabulary | **Read the story. Then answer the questions below using the past perfect.**

Last Tuesday, Peter got ready for his interview with a company called Compu-com. He left class and went to an ATM to get cash, but he didn't have time to get gas. He decided to get it early Wednesday morning. That night, he read over his cover letter and résumé. He felt confident. He always wrote good letters, and he had a great résumé with a nice photo. He had paid a professional to help him put it together.

Before going to bed, he got his things ready: his suit, shirt and tie, his best shoes. He set his alarm for 7:00 and went to sleep. But his cell phone was in silent mode, and he didn't hear it go off. Peter woke up at 8:30, but he left the house in two minutes flat! He didn't have enough gas to drive to Compu-com, so he decided to take a taxi. Of course, they were all occupied. After 15 minutes, a taxi stopped. There was a woman in the backseat. She asked, "Do you want a ride to Compu-com?" Peter didn't know her, but she obviously recognized him.

1. Why was Peter feeling confident?   _He had written a good cover letter and résumé._
2. Why was his résumé very strong?   _____
3. Why did he sleep late on Wednesday morning?   _____
4. Why was he able to leave home so quickly?   _____
5. Why didn't he have enough gas to drive to the interview?   _____
6. Why did he have enough money for a taxi?   _____
7. Had Peter met the woman before?   _____
8. How do you think the woman recognized Peter?   _____

4 About you

Grammar | **Write about a strange experience or coincidence that happened to you or someone you know. Use the simple past and past perfect. Use the ideas in the box or your own ideas.**

You received an email or a text from a friend you were thinking about.
You ran into an old friend on vacation in another part of your country.
You met someone with the same birthday as you.
You found an item that belonged to a friend in a strange place.
You gave a friend or family member the same present that he or she gave you.

_____

_____

_____

_____

_____

_____

1 Super superstitions

Vocabulary | **What superstitions do these pictures illustrate? Write the superstition below each picture.**

1. _If you put your clothes on inside out, you'll get a nice surprise._

2. _____

3. _____

4. _____

5. _____

6. _____

2 More world superstitions

Vocabulary | **Complete the superstitions with the expressions in the box.**

| broom | come into | come true | make | snake | sweep |

1. Thailand: It's lucky to dream of a _____ because it means you'll meet the man or woman of your dreams.

2. China and Vietnam: It's bad luck to _____ the floor on New Year's Day with a _____ . You'll take away your good fortune.

3. Turkey: If you stand between two people with the same name and _____ a wish, your wish will _____ .

4. Ireland: If the palm of your right hand itches, it might mean you'll _____ money.

3 Are you superstitious?

Grammar | **Complete the conversation with responses with *So* and *Neither*.**

Junya   Are you superstitious?

Marta   I'm not sure, actually.

Junya   _Neither am I._

Marta   Do you believe in bad luck?

Junya   Oh, do you mean like believing you'll have bad luck
        if you buy just one pillow? Well, I never buy just one.

Marta   _____

Junya   I mean, I don't believe it's unlucky. Still, I always buy two,
        just in case . . .

Marta   _____ Anyway, why do you ask?

Junya   Well, a friend of mine told me it's unlucky to sneeze only once.

Marta   I didn't know that!

Junya   _____ . . . But I *am* interested in all that stuff.

Marta   _____ . . . So, does that mean we are superstitious, then?

4 I agree! . . . Or do I?

Grammar | **Write two responses to each statement – one response with *So* or *Neither*,
to show you are the same, and another showing you are different.**

1. | I always make a wish when
   I see a falling star. |
   So do I, if I see one.
   Really? I've never heard of that superstition.

2. | I believe in telepathy. |
   _____
   _____

3. | I never cut my fingernails on Fridays. |
   _____
   _____

4. | I always pick up pennies for good luck. |
   _____
   _____

5. | I didn't know it was unlucky to spill salt. |
   _____
   _____

1 Funny and hilarious

Choose the best word to repeat the underlined idea in each sentence.

1. I have the <u>funniest</u> dreams, like one about me teaching a class in my robe and hair curlers. I mean, isn't that **frustrating** / (**hilarious**)?

2. I don't usually dream, so I find other people's dreams <u>interesting</u> to listen to. It's really **fascinating** / **scary** to listen to them.

3. I sometimes have this <u>amazing</u> dream that I can fly. It's just a **comical** / **wonderful** dream.

4. Every once in a while, I have this really <u>scary</u> dream. I'm driving along a road, and suddenly, I don't know how to drive! It's **disappointing** / **frightening**.

5. About once or twice a year, I have this <u>strange</u> dream that I'm back in college taking an important test. I mean, isn't it **weird** / **fascinating** to dream about something like that?

6. I wish I could remember my dreams, but it <u>isn't easy</u>. I mean, it's **difficult** / **important**. I heard you should write them down the moment you wake up.

2 How many ways can you say *beautiful*?

Conversation strategies | Complete each sentence by using a word to repeat the main idea in the first sentence.

1. I often dream about a very attractive woman. She's really ___beautiful___ .

2. She's very easygoing. She's a really _____ kind of person.

3. She never gets annoyed. She never gets _____ .

4. In my dream, we do some fun things together. You know, we do _____ stuff, like play games in the clouds.

5. They're always happy dreams. They're never _____ .

3 Strong or soft

Conversation strategies | Read the comments. Does *just* make what the people say stronger or softer? Write *stronger* or *softer*.

1. I didn't sleep well last night. I guess I just ate too much spicy food before I went to bed. ___softer___

2. Last night, I dreamed I won ten million dollars! It was just the most incredible dream. _____

3. I don't really believe in superstitions. They're just a bit of fun. _____

4. I went to bed early last night. I was just exhausted. _____

5. I had a terrible nightmare last night. It was just the worst dream I've ever had. _____

4 About you

Conversation strategies | Write answers to the questions below. Use *just* to make your answers stronger or softer as necessary.

1. Do you believe in telepathy? *Yes, I do. I think some people can really tell what others are thinking. It's just amazing.* **or** *No, I don't. I just don't believe you can ever tell what others are thinking.*

2. Do you like to watch TV shows about UFOs? _____

3. Do you think you can make something happen by wishing for it? _____

4. Do you believe that aliens exist? _____

5. Do you believe that dreams give us clues about our past or our future? _____

Lesson D / Amazing stories

1 How strange is that?

Reading **A** Read the stories. Write the number of the title that best describes each story.

1. I Really, Really Love You!
2. Special Delivery . . . to Jail
3. Not a Book, but My Daughter
4. Reluctant Movie Star

Would You Believe . . . ?

WOULD YOU BELIEVE . . . ?

☐ Charles McLean, who works for a New York shipping company, wanted to visit his parents but didn't want to spend $320 on a plane ticket. Instead, he packed himself into a shipping crate and express-mailed himself to DeSoto, Texas. When the crate was delivered to his parents' home, he broke out of the box and shook hands with the delivery person. Unfortunately, the frightened woman did not have a sense of humor. She called the police, and McLean was arrested and charged as a stowaway.

☐ Christina Hudson of Denver, Colorado, is such a fan of Stephenie Meyer's *Twilight* books that she changed her name to include all four titles in the series. Hudson is now legally known as Christina Twilight New Moon Eclipse Breaking Dawn Hudson. Christina's mother and father don't mind that she changed her name to honor the *Twilight* books. They are just happy that she didn't choose to rename herself as a series of reality TV shows!

☐ Julianne Clark, a makeup artist at a Hollywood movie studio, was working one Sunday afternoon. When she tried to drive home from the studio, she discovered that the exit gate was locked. As she tried to find another exit, she saw a bus full of people. She followed the bus, thinking it would lead her to an exit. But the bus was part of a movie. Clark followed the bus onto a ramp and slid into a large pool of water after the bus. No one was hurt, but it took security guards three hours to get her car out of the water!

☐ Tim Wilson was worried about being late for his wedding when he crashed his car and broke his arm and leg. Refusing to stay in the hospital, he jumped into a taxi and arrived at the church just in time for the ceremony. But by the time he had cleaned himself up, his painkillers had worn off, and he passed out. He was rushed back to the hospital with his fiancée and the preacher, who married the couple as Wilson lay in his hospital bed.

B Read the article again and answer the questions. Then find words in the article to replace the underlined words.

1. Who couldn't find a way out from her workplace? *an exit* _Julianne Clark_
2. Who was the person that hid on a plane to avoid paying the fare? _____
3. Who took some medicine to stop pain, which then stopped working? _____
4. Who got into a large delivery box? _____
5. Who wanted to show her respect for a series of books? _____

48

2 Happily ever after . . .

Writing **A** Read the story. Add *soon after, after,* or *before*.

Steven Park and his wife Susan were having financial problems. One day, they each decided, without telling the other, to buy a lottery ticket. _____ buying these tickets, they had never spent money on the lottery. They both used numbers that were their anniversary date and address. That night, they were watching the news on TV, and the winning numbers were drawn. _____ hearing the familiar numbers, they started jumping up and down. They were shocked to find out that they each held a winning ticket! The Parks were $450,000 richer _____ picking up their winnings.

B Write an amazing story you know, or make one up. Use prepositional time clauses.

Unit 6 Progress chart

What can you do? Mark the boxes. ✓ = I can . . . ? = I need to review how to . . .	To review, go back to these pages in the Student's Book.
Grammar ☐ use the past perfect.	54 and 55
☐ give responses with *So* and *Neither*.	57
Vocabulary ☐ use at least 12 expressions to describe strange events and superstitions.	54, 55, and 56
Conversation strategies ☐ make my meaning clear by repeating ideas.	58
☐ use *just* to make what I say stronger or softer.	59
Writing ☐ use prepositional time clauses.	61

Illustration credits

Chuck Gonzales: 2, 3, 20, 21, 31, 44, 45, 54, 55, 94 **Frank Montagna:** 10, 11, 26, 27, 46, 47, 52, 67, 76, 78, 79 **Marilena Perilli:** 6, 7, 22, 23, 40, 58, 70, 71, 93 **Greg White:** 18, 38, 61, 69 **Terry Wong:** 12, 13, 28, 29, 50, 62, 63, 83, 90 **Q2A Studio Artists:** 59, 72

Photo credits

4 *(top to bottom)* ©Polka Dot Images/Thinkstock; ©Punchstock; ©Ryan McVay/Thinkstock **5** ©newphotoservice/Shutterstock **8** ©RON EDMONDS/Associated Press **14** ©Getty Images **15** ©Punchstock **16** *(left to right)* ©Mel Curtis/Getty Images/RF; ©Tim Garcha/Corbis; ©Kaz Chiba/Getty Images **18** © Tongro Image Stock/agefotostoc **19** *(top to bottom)* ©Tim Thompson/Corbis; ©David Lyons/Alamy; ©Watt, Elizabeth/agefotostock *(background)* ©Malchev/Shutterstock **24** ©Jim Arbogast/Getty Images/RF **30** ©Zero Creatives/Getty Images **31** ©Westend61/Getty Images/RF **32** ©Ryan McVay/Thinkstock **34** ©Punchstock **42** ©SnowWhiteimages/Shutterstock **49** ©Sean Gladwell/Shutterstock **60** *(top to bottom)* ©Andresr/Shutterstock; ©arek_malang/Shutterstock; © Ocean/Corbis/RF; © photomak/Shutterstock **64** ©ColinCramm/Shutterstock **66** ©SuperStock/agefotostock **67** ©George Doyle/Thinkstock **72** *(books)* ©LanKS/Shutterstock **74** *(top to bottom)* ©Kevork Djansezian/Getty Images; ©Thinkstock/Getty Images; ©PhotoAlto/James Hardy **75** *(top to bottom)* ©Kike Calvo/National Geographic Society/Corbis; ©Lane Oatey/Blue Jean Images/Getty Images/RF; ©Digital Vision/Getty Images; ©Punchstock; ©Wayne Eardley/Masterfile **77** *(top, top to bottom)* ©s_bukley/Shutterstock; ©Helga Esteb/Shutterstock *(bottom, left to right)* ©MGM/courtesy Everett Collection; ©MGM/courtesy Everett Collection; ©20th Century Fox Film Corp/Everett Collection; ©Alexandra Wyman/Getty Images **80** *(left to right)* ©D Dipasupil/FilmMagic/Getty Images; ©Jason LaVeris/FilmMagic/Getty Images *(diamond)* ©pdesign/Shutterstock *(background)* ©Ezepov Dmitry/Shutterstock **85** ©Sue Wilson/Alamy **86** ©Randy Faris/Corbis

Text credits

While every effort has been made, it has not always been possible to identify the sources of all the material used, or to trace all copyright holders. If any omissions are brought to our notice, we will be happy to include the appropriate acknowledgements on reprinting.

The top 500 spoken words

This is a list of the top 500 words in spoken North American English. It is based on a sample of four and a half million words of conversation from the Cambridge International Corpus. The most frequent word, *I*, is at the top of the list.

1. I	40. really	79. see
2. and	41. with	80. how
3. the	42. he	81. they're
4. you	43. one	82. kind
5. uh	44. are	83. here
6. to	45. this	84. from
7. a	46. there	85. did
8. that	47. I'm	86. something
9. it	48. all	87. too
10. of	49. if	88. more
11. yeah	50. no	89. very
12. know	51. get	90. want
13. in	52. about	91. little
14. like	53. at	92. been
15. they	54. out	93. things
16. have	55. had	94. an
17. so	56. then	95. you're
18. was	57. because	96. said
19. but	58. go	97. there's
20. is	59. up	98. I've
21. it's	60. she	99. much
22. we	61. when	100. where
23. huh	62. them	101. two
24. just	63. can	102. thing
25. oh	64. would	103. her
26. do	65. as	104. didn't
27. don't	66. me	105. other
28. that's	67. mean	106. say
29. well	68. some	107. back
30. for	69. good	108. could
31. what	70. got	109. their
32. on	71. OK	110. our
33. think	72. people	111. guess
34. right	73. now	112. yes
35. not	74. going	113. way
36. um	75. were	114. has
37. or	76. lot	115. down
38. my	77. your	116. we're
39. be	78. time	117. any

The top 500 spoken words

118. he's	161. five	204. sort
119. work	162. always	205. great
120. take	163. school	206. bad
121. even	164. look	207. we've
122. those	165. still	208. another
123. over	166. around	209. car
124. probably	167. anything	210. true
125. him	168. kids	211. whole
126. who	169. first	212. whatever
127. put	170. does	213. twenty
128. years	171. need	214. after
129. sure	172. us	215. ever
130. can't	173. should	216. find
131. pretty	174. talking	217. care
132. gonna	175. last	218. better
133. stuff	176. thought	219. hard
134. come	177. doesn't	220. haven't
135. these	178. different	221. trying
136. by	179. money	222. give
137. into	180. long	223. I'd
138. went	181. used	224. problem
139. make	182. getting	225. else
140. than	183. same	226. remember
141. year	184. four	227. might
142. three	185. every	228. again
143. which	186. new	229. pay
144. home	187. everything	230. try
145. will	188. many	231. place
146. nice	189. before	232. part
147. never	190. though	233. let
148. only	191. most	234. keep
149. his	192. tell	235. children
150. doing	193. being	236. anyway
151. cause	194. bit	237. came
152. off	195. house	238. six
153. I'll	196. also	239. family
154. maybe	197. use	240. wasn't
155. real	198. through	241. talk
156. why	199. feel	242. made
157. big	200. course	243. hundred
158. actually	201. what's	244. night
159. she's	202. old	245. call
160. day	203. done	246. saying

The top 500 spoken words

247. dollars	290. started	333. believe
248. live	291. job	334. thinking
249. away	292. says	335. funny
250. either	293. play	336. state
251. read	294. usually	337. until
252. having	295. wow	338. husband
253. far	296. exactly	339. idea
254. watch	297. took	340. name
255. week	298. few	341. seven
256. mhm	299. child	342. together
257. quite	300. thirty	343. each
258. enough	301. buy	344. hear
259. next	302. person	345. help
260. couple	303. working	346. nothing
261. own	304. half	347. parents
262. wouldn't	305. looking	348. room
263. ten	306. someone	349. today
264. interesting	307. coming	350. makes
265. am	308. eight	351. stay
266. sometimes	309. love	352. mom
267. bye	310. everybody	353. sounds
268. seems	311. able	354. change
269. heard	312. we'll	355. understand
270. goes	313. life	356. such
271. called	314. may	357. gone
272. point	315. both	358. system
273. ago	316. type	359. comes
274. while	317. end	360. thank
275. fact	318. least	361. show
276. once	319. told	362. thousand
277. seen	320. saw	363. left
278. wanted	321. college	364. friends
279. isn't	322. ones	365. class
280. start	323. almost	366. already
281. high	324. since	367. eat
282. somebody	325. days	368. small
283. let's	326. couldn't	369. boy
284. times	327. gets	370. paper
285. guy	328. guys	371. world
286. area	329. god	372. best
287. fun	330. country	373. water
288. they've	331. wait	374. myself
289. you've	332. yet	375. run

The top 500 spoken words

376. they'll	418. company	460. sorry
377. won't	419. friend	461. living
378. movie	420. set	462. drive
379. cool	421. minutes	463. outside
380. news	422. morning	464. bring
381. number	423. between	465. easy
382. man	424. music	466. stop
383. basically	425. close	467. percent
384. nine	426. leave	468. hand
385. enjoy	427. wife	469. gosh
386. bought	428. knew	470. top
387. whether	429. pick	471. cut
388. especially	430. important	472. computer
389. taking	431. ask	473. tried
390. sit	432. hour	474. gotten
391. book	433. deal	475. mind
392. fifty	434. mine	476. business
393. months	435. reason	477. anybody
394. women	436. credit	478. takes
395. month	437. dog	479. aren't
396. found	438. group	480. question
397. side	439. turn	481. rather
398. food	440. making	482. twelve
399. looks	441. American	483. phone
400. summer	442. weeks	484. program
401. hmm	443. certain	485. without
402. fine	444. less	486. moved
403. hey	445. must	487. gave
404. student	446. dad	488. yep
405. agree	447. during	489. case
406. mother	448. lived	490. looked
407. problems	449. forty	491. certainly
408. city	450. air	492. talked
409. second	451. government	493. beautiful
410. definitely	452. eighty	494. card
411. spend	453. wonderful	495. walk
412. happened	454. seem	496. married
413. hours	455. wrong	497. anymore
414. war	456. young	498. you'll
415. matter	457. places	499. middle
416. supposed	458. girl	500. tax
417. worked	459. happen	